IØ116154

CULTURAL DIPLOMACY

No Bullet, No Blood

A Transformative Force to
Advance Understanding and Dialogue

SECTION ONE:

The Importance of Culture and Creative Industry

SECTION TWO:

Cultural Diplomacy: A Comprehensive Essay

SECTION THREE:

Cultural Diplomacy: The Essential Skills

Author: Mosi Dorbayani

Cover Design by: Christelle Walker
Cover Image: Girl in Military Uniform, Playing Balalaika (WWII).

WAALM Publications, 2019, 2025
Library and Archives Canada

ISBN: 978-0-9940842-8-6

This book is dedicated to you.

CONTENTS

Foreword   1

SECTION ONE

The Importance of Culture and Creative Industry

Introduction   6

Impact of Culture on Health   8

Impact of Culture & Creative Industry on Economy   11

Impact of Cultural Practice on Tolerance and Understanding   14

Impact of Culture & Creative Industry on Democracy   18

No Bullet, No Blood   19

SECTION TWO

Cultural Diplomacy: A Comprehensive Essay

Introduction   24

Definition   22

Purpose   27

Tools of Cultural Diplomacy   30

Challenges   31

CHAPTER 1

Music for Cultural Diplomacy   35

CHAPTER 2

Film for Cultural Diplomacy   49

CHAPTER 3

Theater and Performing Arts for Cultural Diplomacy   58

CHAPTER 4

Fine Art for Cultural Diplomacy 69

CHAPTER 5

Aboriginal Arts for Cultural Diplomacy 72

CHAPTER 6

Poetry for Cultural Diplomacy 78

CHAPTER 7

TV Shows for Cultural Diplomacy 82

CHAPTER 8

Digital for Cultural Diplomacy 84

SECTION THREE

Cultural Diplomacy: The Essential Quality and Skills

Who is a Cultural Diplomat? 89

The Key Qualities of a Cultural Diplomat 90

The Skill Sets of a Cultural Diplomat 91

ABOUT AUTHOR 95

REFERENCES 104

"In pursuit of cultural diplomacy, it's imperative to get the balance between persuasion and assertion right."

Author

FOREWORD

Culture lies at the core of human development and civilization. Long before nations established economic or trade relationships, art, literature, and music served as unifying forces across borders. Centuries of creative expression, migratory flows, and intercultural exchange enriched shared values globally. Such cultural cross-pollination fostered mutual understanding and norms that have often paved the way for peace, stability, prosperity, and solidarity.

Today, cultural exchanges remain as dynamic as ever. Modern communication technologies have dramatically expanded the reach of cultural activities, propelling the demand for cultural goods at an unprecedented pace. Globalization has heightened exposure to diverse cultures, deepening our curiosity, enhancing our creativity and imagination, and broadening our capacity to engage with—and benefit from—other cultures. This has cultivated a deeper appreciation for their contributions to the rich diversity of our societies.

While culture is frequently associated with fine arts— including visual art, literature, cultural goods, and services— it also encompasses an anthropological dimension rooted in meanings, beliefs, values, and traditions. These are expressed

1

through language, religion, mythology, and artistic forms. Thus, culture plays not only a strategic role in human advancement but also a vital role in deciphering the intricate mosaic of identities, customs, and behavioral patterns within individuals and communities.

Culture exemplifies "soft power"—an influential force derived from values such as human dignity, solidarity, tolerance, freedom of expression, respect for diversity, and intercultural dialogue. When these principles are upheld, they have the capacity to yield profound benefits for humanity.

From a political standpoint, there is growing recognition that culture is a critical instrument for achieving strategic objectives related to prosperity, cohesion, and security. Economically, the cultural sector already constitutes a vibrant driver of activity and employment—particularly within North America and Europe.

Cultural initiatives frequently promote social inclusion, celebrate diversity, and play a role in alleviating physical and psychological deprivation. Creative entrepreneurs, artists, writers, performers, and the thriving cultural industries they fuel represent a wellspring of innovation and sustainability for future generations.

Such immense potential warrants further recognition and full exploration by both cultural practitioners and government institutions.

To foster deeper understanding, this book encapsulates the significance of cross-cultural interaction and presents compelling insights into the essential role of *Cultural Diplomacy*.

"Cultural exchange gives us the chance to appreciate points of commonality, and where there are differences, to understand the motivations and humanity that underlie them"

Rachel Briggs, OBE

SECTION ONE

The Importance of Culture & Creative Industry

Introduction

In the wake of the global financial crisis, the world continues to grapple with deepening social inequality, mass immigration, increasingly diverse populations, and the rise of extremism, radicalization, and multifaceted threats. Disruptive strategies, along with rapid advancements in technology and digital communication, are reshaping societies—altering lifestyles, shifting consumer behaviors, and recalibrating the balance of economic power, political stability, and the global order.

Amidst this volatile and evolving landscape, the role of culture has become more vital than ever. Harnessing the full potential of culture offers a powerful pathway toward building a more inclusive and equitable world—one where innovation, creativity, sustainability, and shared growth are attainable for all.

Culture fosters active citizenship and encourages intercultural dialogue, both within nations and across international boundaries. It empowers individuals and strengthens the social fabric by promoting cohesion and solidarity. Culture serves as a unifying thread that draws communities closer, integrates refugees and other migrants, and cultivates a sense of belonging.

Furthermore, **culture and the creative industries** possess a transformative capacity to improve lives, revitalize communities, stimulate employment, and spur economic growth. Their influence reverberates beyond the cultural sector, permeating other areas of the economy and contributing to overall societal progress.

Impact of Culture on Health

Cultural participation plays a significant role in enhancing health and overall well-being. In Canada, the *Access and Availability Survey (2018)* revealed that nearly three-quarters (73%) of permanent immigrants consider arts and culture to be at least moderately important to their quality of life and that of their family—a sentiment shared by 68% of the Canadian-born population (www.capacoa.ca). Across Europe, cultural proximity has also shown notable psychological benefits. According to a recent *Eurobarometer* survey, 71% of Europeans agreed that "living close to places related to cultural heritage can improve quality of life" (www.europarl.europa.eu). Engagement in cultural experiences—such as attending theaters, music concerts, or cultural festivals—has been strongly linked to positive health outcomes. Research indicates that individuals participating in such activities are up to 32% more likely to report excellent or very good health, even after adjusting for external factors (www.hillstrategies.com). Additional findings show that regular attendees of concerts, theater, and cinema exhibit lower levels of anxiety, experience reduced depression, and generally enjoy better physical and mental health (Cuypers, 2011, p.6).

8

The frequency of participation in performing and receptive arts correlates directly with self-reported good health, as supported by studies from Wilkinson (2007) and *CAPACOA* (www.capacoa.ca). Moreover, attending live cultural events has been shown to increase perceived vitality and energy (Bygren, 2009). For children and youth, engagement in cultural activities has profound developmental benefits. It nurtures cognitive growth, strengthens self-esteem, and bolsters resilience—all of which contribute meaningfully to improved educational outcomes.

Evidence suggests that arts participation is particularly impactful for students from disadvantaged backgrounds. According to findings by the *Cultural Learning Alliance*, pupils from low-income families who are actively involved in school-based arts programs are three times more likely to attain a university degree compared to their peers who lack such exposure (www.culturallearningalliance.org.uk).

Happy Children, Enjoying the Colors of India on Their Faces – Holi Fest.

Cultural Participation, Public Dance - Lima, Peru

Impact of Culture & Creative Industry on Economy

Culture and creativity are indispensable assets in any modern economy. Culture contributes directly to employment, economic growth, and international trade, while creativity fuels innovation across sectors striving to maintain a competitive edge.

A cornerstone role of the creative industry lies in cultivating partnerships throughout the community. In Canada, this collaborative spirit is clearly reflected: 86% of creative organizations partner with other arts institutions, 84% engage with a broad spectrum of community groups, 78% collaborate with schools and educational institutions, 67% connect with government bodies, and 64% engage the private sector (Survey of Performing Arts Presenters, www.capacoa.ca).

Artists and creative professionals frequently lead these partnerships, and 82% believe that continuing collaboration within the industry and with community organizations will be vital over the coming decade. This collective effort not only strengthens social and cultural frameworks but also drives resilience and innovation within local economies.

Beyond partnerships, capital investments also illustrate the sector's economic significance. Between 2012 and 2017, 114

Canadian creative organizations invested an impressive $442.5 million, underscoring culture's tangible and strategic contribution to national economic development (Survey of Performing Arts Presenters, www.capacoa.ca).

Of course, Gunshi! Here's a polished and elevated version of your text, with enhanced fluency and sophistication—while maintaining all original keywords, data points, and citations:

The Performing Arts sector alone makes a significant contribution to Canada's economy. In 2016, it added $2.7 billion to the nation's Gross Domestic Product (GDP) and supported approximately 65,000 jobs, underscoring its role as a vital economic driver.

International interest in Canada's cultural landscape also translates into considerable financial impact. That same year, foreign visitors spent $220 million directly on live performance events—$188 million on performing arts and $32 million on festivals and celebrations. This accounts for 1.1% of total tourism spending and 6.4% of non-tourism commodities—which include expenditures outside of travel, accommodation, and food (Statistics Canada, www.statcan.gc.ca, 2018).

Beyond its financial value, the presence of a vibrant arts and culture scene is viewed as a strategic asset in workforce and business development. 65% of businesses and skilled professionals in Canada identify a thriving cultural environment as a key consideration when evaluating relocation opportunities (Statistics Canada, www.statcan.gc.ca).

Urban and rural communities alike are increasingly recognizing the strategic value of culture and the cultural industries as catalysts for economic and social vitality. These sectors play a pivotal role in attracting investment, drawing employers, engaging students, and welcoming tourists.

By integrating the specialized knowledge and creative skills inherent in cultural fields with expertise from other industries, communities foster innovative, cross-sector solutions. This dynamic fusion generates new opportunities across diverse domains—including information and communication technologies, travel and tourism, manufacturing, retail, and service industries—advancing both economic development and cultural enrichment.

Impact of Cultural Practice on Tolerance & Understanding

Culture Track Canada explored perceptions of arts and culture with an open-ended question: "What is the greatest impact a cultural organization can have on your world?" Citizens born in Canada and new Canadians reported the same top two impact:

- New ideas/broaden experiences.
- Knowledge of/understanding other cultures. (Culture Track Canada, www.culturetrack.com)

UNESCO's Declaration of Principles on Tolerance (1995) defines tolerance as "the respect, acceptance, and appreciation of the rich diversity of our world's cultures, our forms of expression and ways of being human." This foundational perspective underscores that tolerance is cultivated through openness, dialogue, and the unwavering protection of freedom of expression and thought.

Since tolerance entails sustaining harmony amidst diversity, **the** cultural and creative industries serve as vital agents in promoting it. Through the lens of artistic expression and cultural exchange, they foster empathy, challenge prejudice, and bridge divides—making space for diverse voices and narratives.

Without tolerance and mutual understanding, peace remains elusive. Cultural practitioners and creative sectors possess the unique capacity to forge common ground for dialogue, social engagement, and the continued evolution of a "culture of peace" on a global scale.

Cultural activities strengthen communities and facilitate understanding among groups. They give people a greater sense of cohesion and lead them to develop more positive attitudes about their shared environment.

According to Tim Kaseer, PhD in Psychology: "Culture is about identity and difference as well as the 'common experiences' that make us human." The arts and culture can provide disruptive experiences that may "act as catalysts to help some people identify the truly meaningful and satisfying values around which to orient their lives". (www.hillstrategies.com)

'Understanding is a virtue that makes peace and prosperity possible'.

Developing genuine understanding requires guidance. We often need support to explore diverse ways of life, modes of thought, behavioral patterns, and attitudes. Given that culture is intricately linked to human behavior—a phenomenon both deeply complex and worthy of thorough investigation—fields such as anthropology and psychology play a pivotal role in advancing this exploration. Engaging with cultural studies and participating in cultural activities can help us derive meaning and foster a deeper comprehension of the human experience. Importantly, the creative industries and cultural institutions serve as key enablers, equipping individuals and communities with the knowledge, tools, and exposure necessary to cultivate intercultural understanding.

Author is signing International Memorandum of Cultural Exchange & Dialogue. Grand Royal, Budapest, Hungary – EU.

Culture is learned behavior. It is an inseparable part of people's lives, shaping their perceptions, values, sense of humor, worldview, and emotional landscape—including their aspirations, loyalties, concerns, and fears. Thus, when we engage with others and build relationships, acquiring cultural awareness becomes essential. It not only deepens empathy and mutual respect but also increases our capacity for tolerance— laying the foundation for authentic human connection.

Impact of Culture and Creative Industry on Democracy

One of democracy's most essential functions is its ability to facilitate political change and resolve ideological differences without resorting to violence. Consequently, its foundational principles are inseparably linked to a constellation of values: peace, tolerance, and human rights. For these values to flourish meaningfully, culture—and the deliberate cultivation of a culture of peace—must be embedded at democracy's core.

In this context, the voices of artists, writers, and members of the creative industries hold particular significance. Though they may challenge political objectives—or even offer conflicting perspectives—they illuminate concerns that public officials might overlook or hesitate to advance. These creative voices articulate truths that resonate deeply with the hearts and minds of communities, touching not only national consciousness but the broader human experience.

Above all, freedom of thought and freedom of expression, and the unimpeded right of cultural practitioners to exercise them, serve as cornerstones in safeguarding democratic systems. In fostering open dialogue, critical reflection, and cultural expression, they ensure democracy remains vibrant, inclusive, and responsive to the needs of its people.

No Bullet, No Blood

Culture's soft power holds transformative potential in shaping global diplomacy. History has shown us time and again that there is no enduring military solution to conflict—dialogue and diplomacy remain the only guarantees of lasting peace. To preserve peace, stability, and global order, strength may serve as a deterrent, but it is tact and diplomacy that most effectively uphold the principles of coexistence.

Within this framework, cultural diplomacy and the strategic use of soft power can cultivate trust—across borders, political divides, and cultural differences. By offering shared spaces for cooperation and mutual understanding, they enable individuals and communities to engage meaningfully, even when official relations are strained or severed. Such initiatives can reopen diplomatic pathways, where dialogue had once faltered.

Though perspectives vary among diplomats, scholars, and authors, many distinguish between organic cultural relations, which evolve naturally without state involvement, and cultural diplomacy, a term they reserve for government-led efforts executed through official diplomatic channels.

The challenge in drawing rigid lines between cultural relations and cultural diplomacy lies in overlooking a fundamental truth: it is not government officials or political envoys who craft the lifeblood of cultural exchange—it is the artists, writers, performers, and the broader creative community who do so. These voices, often independent and impassioned, are the true ambassadors of empathy and understanding. They embody the spirit of cultural diplomacy far more authentically than any official emissary.

Helena K. Finn (2003), a senior American diplomat, reminds us that during the early Cold War, U.S. policymakers grasped the strategic power of engaging foreign publics—and recognized cultural diplomacy as vital to national security. At the time, efforts to advance this vision were backed by the CIA and the State Department's Division of Cultural Relations. While such sponsorships would now be rightly deemed inappropriate and counterproductive, this historical precedent underscores how seriously cultural exchange was once treated—as a frontline strategy in promoting mutual understanding.

Yet today, such initiatives are alarmingly de-emphasized. In an era where diplomacy is too often eclipsed by militarism, the profound role of cultural engagement is being steadily marginalized—a sobering trend when many policymakers still default to force as the primary response to ideological radicalism.

SECTION TWO

Cultural Diplomacy: A Comprehensive Essay

"Without culture, and the relative freedom it implies, society, even when perfect, is but a jungle. This is why any authentic creation is a gift to the future."

Albert Camus

Introduction

Though the term "cultural diplomacy" is relatively modern, its practice stretches deep into the annals of history. Long before formal recognition, it was embodied by pilgrims, explorers, merchants, educators, and artists—individuals who served as informal envoys, forging connections across cultural boundaries. These figures were, in essence, early cultural ambassadors, carrying with them ideas, artistry, and ways of life that shaped encounters between distant societies. Cultural exchange arises wherever people engage across difference—through art, sport, literature, music, science, commerce, and beyond. Every act of cross-cultural communication fosters mutual understanding, often weaving stronger threads into the fabric of society. The historic interplay of languages, religions, philosophies, and artistic traditions has long enriched global relationships, cultivating shared values and more resilient social structures. Today, cultural diplomacy stands not only as a dynamic concept in global affairs but also as a vibrant and innovative academic discipline—one that continues to evolve as both theory and practice. It offers a powerful lens through which to interpret history and imagine futures shaped by empathy, dialogue, and creativity. (www.culturaldiplomacy.org)

Definition

France began employing the term "cultural diplomacy" as early as the late nineteenth century, although it only gained widespread use in international discourse during the 1990s. Initially, the term described state-led initiatives—diplomats using cultural exchanges to advance their nations' strategic interests. Over time, however, its definition expanded to encompass the broader exchange of ideas, arts, and cultural practices between countries and their peoples, serving the purpose of fostering mutual understanding (Cummings, 2003, p.1).

Joseph S. Nye (2004, p.18) famously conceptualized cultural diplomacy as a facet of "Soft Power"—the ability to achieve desired outcomes not through coercion, but through attraction. This kind of influence emerges from a nation's cultural richness, political ideals, and societal practices, reinforcing the notion that culture holds measurable power in shaping international perceptions.

Moreover, cultural diplomacy is often considered a vital component of public diplomacy—a form of engagement enhanced by civil society itself. As Carnes (2006, p.15) observes, public diplomacy serves to "amplify and publicize the society and its culture to the world," giving voice to a nation through its people, rather than merely through policy.

The term 'Soft Power,' was coined by the Harvard political scientist, Joseph Nye in 1990. Since then, it has overshadowed international relations and public diplomacy. It distinguishes the command or hard power – economic carrots and military sticks, from 'soft' power of 'getting others to want what you want.

Here I define cultural diplomacy as:

The art of initiating dialogue through exchange of ideas and creations to soften dispute, political disagreement and military conflict – an artistry to reinforce mutual understanding, foster socio-economic collaboration and ties to advance regional and national interests.

Author, Addressing Cultural Representatives from 10 Countries, London, England.

Cultural diplomacy may be practised by general public, private sector, civil society, or even by those holding offices in a 'responsible government'.

Purpose

Ultimately, the main objective of cultural diplomacy is to advance mutual understanding.

It may serve to sway an international audience and to utilize that impact, which is developed over the long haul, as a kind of positive attitude hold to bolster policies. It tries to outfit the components of culture to prompt outsiders to:

- Have a constructive perspective of the country's kin, culture and approaches,
- Ignite more noteworthy collaboration between the two countries,
- Facilitate change in strategies or political conditions.
  (Michael, 2009 p.77)

Cultural diplomacy, when properly learned and connected at all dimensions, not only has the novel capacity to impact the 'world public sentiment', but also the 'belief system of people, their networks, and their countries'.

Cultural diplomacy can indeed facilitate and quicken the acknowledgment of:

- Worldwide intercultural discourse;
- Global intercultural dialogue;

27

- Justice;
- Association, collaboration and understanding;
- The assurance of human rights;
- World peace and harmony.

Simon Brault, Vice-Chair of the Canada Council for the Arts, and the president of Culture Montréal in his recent speech (2018) at Cercle France-Amériques mentioned: "Cultural diplomacy changes, adapts, expands and contracts in response to shifting political regimes and situational requirements. Fortunately, it never goes away altogether. That's because it is based on long-standing traditions, and because culture will always be there to come to the rescue when humanity is under threat." (www.canadacouncil.ca)

Philosophers, wise policymakers, and smart political leaders have long realized the power that entails from having a debate and forging dialogue. Creative industry in any given culture has that unique power to softly engage people. One may use the language of music, the other, the power of silver screen; one may engage audience on stage, while the other trigger them through words. Regardless of instrument, the purpose is the same – to server the betterment of humanity, especially during the crisis.

A Dance Performance by Award Winning Performer, 'Neysham', from USA at
WAALM Awards.

Tools of Cultural Diplomacy

Michael Waller, Author and VP of Government Relations, Center for Security Policy explains that cultural diplomacy can and utilizes each part of a nation's culture. (Waller, 2009, p82-87) This includes:

- Expressions of the human experience including films, music, painting, theater, design, etc.
- Exhibitions and shows which offer the possibility to feature various objects of culture.
- Instructive programs, e.g. formal classes, seminars, international student exchange.
- News and Cultural Broadcast.
- Religious diplomacy, including inter-faith discourse.
- Research and advancement of ideas and social policies.

The above tools try to establish an understanding of a nation's culture for its international audiences and they work best, when they are significant to the intended audience. Thus, this entails a clear understanding of the crowd and public behavior. Generally, these tools are not made by an administration, but rather created by the culture and after that the government eases their exhibition abroad with the aim to create an impact. (Mark, Sep/Oct 2002, p.51, 52)

Challenges

Governments seeking to administer cultural diplomacy programs often face a distinct set of challenges. Chief among these is their limited ability to influence the practices and cultural landscapes of foreign nations. Additionally, national administrations are rarely the originators of the cultural products—films, books, music, television—that circulate internationally. Their primary role, rather than direct creation, is to cultivate pathways for these cultural expressions to reach foreign audiences (Mark, 2002, p.50).

As Louis Bélanger of Laval University argues, for governments to remain culturally relevant in an era defined by globalization, they must exert some degree of control over the flows of information and exchange (Bélanger, 1999, p.677–678). However, such control proves difficult within a free-market context. In democratic societies, the state typically does not dominate the majority of data streams. What governments can do, however, is support cultural exports through international trade agreements or facilitate access to foreign broadcasting platforms, thereby expanding reach and influence.

That said, government involvement in cultural diplomacy is not without peril. There lies the temptation to weaponize cultural products—to manipulate content in service of state propaganda rather than genuine intercultural dialogue. This risk underscores the delicate balance between state support and artistic autonomy in the pursuit of meaningful cultural exchange.

Of course, challenges are not limited to governments. Independent artists, writers, producers and creative institutions often face financial struggles.

Princesses of Violin, Award Winners in Classical Music for Spreading Love and Peace around the world.

Grants and scholarships are limited. Copyright and loyalties have different interpretations in different parts of the world. And sadly, media publicity is often given to those who are signed commercially by major labels/studios – who are already in the limelight.

Dr. John Curtis, OBE of The British Museum, Signing International Memorandum of Cultural Exchange & Dialogue.

Ren H. Carothers, Award Winning Writer, Signing International Memorandum of Cultural Exchange & Dialogue.

CHAPTER 1

Music for Cultural Diplomacy

Every nation carries its own unique musical heritage—an enduring tapestry of sound woven through history and emotion. One need not be a trained musician or lyricist to appreciate this extraordinary craft, nor to admire the world's masterful composers and songwriters. Music transcends boundaries; it speaks in harmonies and pulses that reach all of us, regardless of background or origin.

Wherever you find yourself—on any corner of this vibrant planet—you possess the innate ability to recognize and respond to the universal language of music. It resonates in our hearts, evokes memory, inspires unity, and reminds us that creativity and connection are deeply human forces.

It is virtually impossible to discuss culture without acknowledging music—a form of artistic expression that resonates profoundly within every society. Music not only embodies the spirit of a culture, but it often serves as the most vivid and enduring representation of its values, stories, and emotional depth. Indeed, the cultural stature of a nation is frequently gauged by its musical legacy and literary contributions to the sonic arts.

Moreover, music serves as a unique conduit between politics and culture. This powerful intersection—when thoughtfully and intentionally employed—has the potential to foster unity across borders and ideologies. As Oana (2016, p.195) insightfully asserts, "this linkage can shape a United World Community," illuminating music's capacity to transcend national interests and forge bonds grounded in shared human experience.

Music stands as a transformative medium through which individuals and nations can communicate, connect, and cultivate meaningful relationships. Its capacity for social cohesion is deeply embedded in its historical and structural evolution. Yet beyond its artistic essence, music has long served as a strategic instrument for advancing political, diplomatic, and societal objectives.

This dynamic role of music in global affairs became especially pronounced during the Cold War era (1947–1991), when it was harnessed as a tool of cultural diplomacy. During this period, American jazz ambassadors, supported by the U.S. State Department, toured internationally to promote values of freedom and personal expression, countering Soviet narratives through the universal language of sound. As noted by the

Institute for Cultural Diplomacy, music emerged as a neutral platform for dialogue, protest, and ideological exchange, capable of bridging divides and fostering mutual understanding. (www.culturaldiplomacy.org , Music as cultural diplomacy, n.d)

In 1954, President Dwight D. Eisenhower appealed for funding from the House Committee on Appropriations with the purpose of countering Communist propaganda with the off-shore display of American exceptionalism. The approved funding was dispersed across multiple government agencies, but more than two-million dollars was allocated to the State Department for the presentation and promotion of American theater, music, dance and some sporting events. The U.S. State Department's original Jazz Ambassadors Program officially began in 1956 and continued into the late 1970s. The program, beyond that point, continued through the Bureau of Educational and Cultural Affairs in the U.S. State Department, working in partnership with the John F. Kennedy Center for the Performing Arts." (www.allaboutjazz.com)

Since the end of the World War II, there have been numerous effective demonstrations of music as Cultural Diplomacy.

Especially since the early 50s, music has helped the humanity to push for peace, to advance harmony, balance and human rights, and has served to tide associations amongst various cultures, nations, and religions.

Here are some notable examples as listed by Oana (2016, p.196-198), adopted by the ICD - Academy for Cultural Diplomacy.

- **1947**, Langollen International Eisteddfood Music Festival: First International Music Festival Held in Wales.
- **1956 - 1970s**, The US' Jazz Ambassadors: The soul of a nation expressed through music.
- **1956**, Eurovision song contest: Contest for the most popular song in Europe, held in Lugano, Switzerland.
- **1958**, International Tchaikovski Piano Competition: Van Cliburn wins the first international Tchaikovski Piano competition, held in Moscow.
- **1963**, The Philippine Madrigal Singers: Promoting cultural diversity, intercultural dialogue and the culture of peace, held in Philippines.
- **1969**, Woodstock Music Festival: the 1960's artists for Peace and Love gathered and performed in Bethel, New York, USA.

- **1969**, John Lennon and Yoko Ono's "Bed-in for Peace" - Hotel Room Peace Campaign, in the midst of Vietnam War, held in Amsterdam, Netherlands.
- **1971**, Rodriguez's 'Cold Fact': Rodriguez's music during the Anti-apartheid movement in South Africa.
- **1976**, Rock Against Racism: Superstars performed together in the UK to stop extremism.
- **1981**, Seattle Peace Concerts: "No speeches, No Preaches".
- **1982**, 'Ein Bisschen Frieden', wins Eurovision Song Contest, the lyrics of the song advocated world peace.
- **1985**, 'We Are the World': Benefit Single for African Famine Relief, written by: Michael Jackson and Lionel Richie .
- **1985**, Life aid, 'Global Jukebox': It raised funds for relief of Ethiopian Famine.
- **1986**, The Human Rights Concerts: Awareness of Amnesty International – acts included Bruce Springsteen, Sting, and U2
- **1987**, China Disabled People's Performing Art Troupe: Toured all over China and in about 40 countries to bring awareness on mental disabilities.

- **1989**, Human Rights Now: Moscow Music Peace Festival, promoting global peace and fighting the drug war in Russia through hard rock music.
- **1992**, Vedran Smailovic Concert: During Balkan War, Cellist from Sarajevo playing in War Ruins
- **1995**, The World Orchestra for Peace: An expression of harmony on all levels.
- **1999**, Peace and Love Festival, Diversity, Solidarity and Understanding, held in Havana, Cuba.
- **1999**, West Eastern Divan Orchestra, Equal in Music: Israeli, Palestinian and other Arab musicians met in Germany to promote social equality.
- **1999**, Musician without Borders: Created in Amsterdam, Netherlands, using the power of music for unity.
- **2000**, The Music 4 Peace Foundation: Formed by Tobias Huber with the aim to spread peace through cultural exchange
- **2004**, Playing for Change: This project came from a common belief that music has the power to break down boundaries and overcome distances between people.
- **2005**, The Rhythm Road: American music abroad, US Jazz Diplomacy in the Post-Cold War era.

- **2006**, Dancing to Connect: an American – Netherlands imitative to connecting the world through dance.
- **2007**, Beating Wing Orchestra, Music collective of refugee and migrant artists.
- **2009**, I Love Hip Hop: The first Hip-Hop Festival in Morocco brining artists together to celebrate unity, and free speech.
- **2010**, The Human Rights Orchestra, one of the major initiative of Musicians for Human Rights. It is a worldwide network of musicians who promote a culture of human rights and social engagement. Founded in 2009 by world-renowned horn player Alessio Allegrini
- **2012**, Chimes of Freedom, Honoring 50 Years of Amnesty International and its work for humanity.
- **2013**, Peace One Day Celebration Concert: Uniting People for Peace, in The Hague, Netherlands.
- **2013**, DMZ World Peace Concert: Facilitating dialogue between North and South Korea.
- **2013**, Atizilut Concert for Peace: Bringing Jewish and Arab Musicians Together. (www.culturaldiplomacy.org)

Hereby, I add to the list:

41

- **2014**, Ottoman Band: Performed in Jaffa, Israel. The performance was an opportunity to showcase and foster strong cultural ties between the two countries.
- **2015**, PANAMANIA Arts and Culture: more than 250 unique performances took place across Toronto from July 10 to August 15 to showcase the diverse cultures of Canada and the Americas through music and dance. It featured 40 national and international performances.
- **2016**, Sound Ports Festival: It was a musical even in Tel Aviv to foster economic and cultural ties between two capitals in Middle East, Istanbul and Tel Aviv. This event established an opportunity for the citizens of the two countries to blend and explore each other's culture and music far from religious differences.
- **2017**, One Love Manchester Concert: It was a benefit concert and British television special held on 4 June, which was organized by American singer Ariana Grande in response to the bombing after her concert at Manchester Arena two weeks earlier. One Love Manchester sent a strong message to the world that "Hatred will never win, fear will never divide us."
- **2018**, Humanities Festival – Vienna: The theme was "Power and Powerlessness", addressing the current

crisis of democracy, the rise of fundamentalists and radical forces, and its search for possible alternatives through artistic and cultural discussions. Participance enjoyed over 40 concerts, films and lectures, half of which were in the English language.

- **2019**, Venezuela Aid Live: It was a humanitarian / aid concert held on 22 Feb in Cúcuta, Colombia, a city near the Venezuelan border. Organized by Richard Branson and Bruno Ocampo and featured over thirty of the best-known Latin American artists from nine countries.

The concert's slogan was, "Let the stars shine for all". The purpose of the concert was to raise money and to pressure Nicolás Maduro to open Venezuela's border for receiving humanitarian aid gathered at its border.

Some other notable examples of music for diplomacy are put together by the USC Center on Public Diplomacy (www.uscpublicdiplomacy.org), which includes but not limited to:

Cotton Club Singers, Performing Jazz Songs at WAALM Awards.

The U.S Jazz Ambassadors: These ambassadors were sponsored by the U.S. State department for over 20 years from the 1956 to the late 1970's. The State department trusted that displaying mainstream American music around the world would acquaint gatherings of people with American culture, as well as win them over as ideological partners exposed to the cold war. The Brubeck Group of Quartet's 12 shows in Poland were some of the first in a long tour that could never stray a way from the edge of the Soviet Association. They went through Eastern Europe, the Middle East, Central Asia and the Indian subcontinent. Different tours permitted Jazz legends like Louis Armstrong and Tipsy Gillespie to trumpet American qualities in recently decolonized states in Africa and Asia. The aim was the same and it was to keep socialism under control. (Perrigo, 2011, www.time.com)

Van Cliburn's Victory in Russia: According to the USC Center on Public Diplomacy, Van Cliburn an American pianist won the first international Tchaikovsky Piano Competition in Moscow in 1958. He was adored by Russian audiences even though he was tagged with an "enemy" status. This was a classic example fortuitous diplomacy.

The Beatles on Our World: A TV special titled "Our world" was broadcasted in 1967. It was the first main live TV programme which featured artists ranging the Beatles to Maria Callas from fourteen different countries across five continents. Their aim was to advance a quiet logic and philosophy amidst the Vietnam War. The Beatles composed and played out "All You Need Is Love." This show boasted the greatest television audience to-date with approximately 400 million individuals tuning in around the globe. (USC Center on Public Diplomacy)

Wham! Freedom Tour goes to China: China's first pop concert was performed by Wham! in Beijing, 1984. Regardless of the tepid gathering from the crowd, this introduction to the Brit-team was a huge moment in UK-China cultural trade. (USC Center on Public Diplomacy).

Moreover, the following recent musical projects raised the bars for social responsibility, understanding and tolerance. They could effectively create dialogue and forums amongst nations on social media worldwide:

Walk in Style: One of the biggest musical projects for humanity, conducted by WAALM, UK and Canada in 2014. Artists from 25 countries, spanning 5 continents shared their talents and voices to fight bullying. An important social issue worldwide, which still causes thousands of victims to commit suicide every year. 'Walk in Style' - the message song to victims of bullying, was written by Canadian songwriter, Mosi Dorbayani, which was recorded in several languages and composed in more than 10 genres. This international project could unite artists and their fans around the world to join forces and establish forums and discussions on this issue on social media worldwide. (https://musicforhumanity.wixsite.com/walkinstyle)

Hopes in Chain: Yet another biggest socially conscious message song honoring Black Lives Matter – Voiced by Yaya Diamond; Songwriter: Mosi Dorbayani

Songs Promoting the UN's International Days:

➢ **'To Whom It May Concern'** - Vocalist: Kate Todd; Songwriter: Mosi Dorbayani & Saadi; Producer: Peter Linseman. This song promotes February 20th, the United Nations' World Day of Social Justice and Equality.

➢ **'May Happiness Pair with You'** - Vocalist: Katie Wiseman; Songwriter: Mosi Dorbayani. This song celebrates and promotes March 20th, the UN's International Day of Happiness.

➢ **'Happiness Is the News!'** - Vocalist: Carla Sacco; Songwriter: Mosi Dorbayani; Producers: Peter Linseman & Carla Sacco. This song supports April 29th the UNESCO's International Dance Day.

➢ **'Madiba'** - Vocalist: Nasambu; Songwriter: Mosi Dorbayani. This song honors July 18th, the UN's

Nelson Mandela Day, and it reminds listeners the importance of human rights and dignity.

➤ **'Oh, You My Friend'** - Vocalist: Krista Earle; Songwriter: Mosi Dorbayani; Arranger: Andysh. This song highlights July 30th, the UN's International Day of Friendship.

➤ **'Chase the Sun'** - Vocalist: Dolly Thompson; Songwriter: Mosi Dorbayani; Orchestration: Makai Symphony. This song celebrates Sep 21st, the UN's Peace Day.

All the above titles are the examples of how music has been used to foster understanding, dialogue and cultural diplomacy throughout the world.

CHAPTER 2

Film for Cultural Diplomacy

The utilization of film in cultural diplomacy is to promote the understanding of the qualities and culture that have place in a nation. For instance, most, if not every, Hollywood movies feature the good life and the American Dream. (Narinehgh, 2012, www.publicandculturaldiplomacy3.wordpress.com)

Film has the capacity to figment life and reality and open up new and obscure views onto the world. To those from other societies or parts of world, films can be taken as the exact delineations of life as projected by its producer.

Film is an incredibly amazing medium; it can portray human, their condition and their rights, and through its narratives, it can make everyone to relate to a situation or an issue. It can potentially unite individuals and create discussions. Through social dialogue, change can gradually appear.

Film can encourage the development of civil society, shared collaboration and understanding, filling in as an adaptable – all around acknowledged vehicle for rapprochement, even with nations where conciliatory relations have been stressed or are missing. (www.culturaldiplomacy.org)

Authors, Gardel and Medavoy (2009) and MacCann (1969) suggest that U.S. cinema and foreign policy have been laced for quite some time, from the World War II screenings in Europe to Cold War film trades which were anti Soviets. Nowadays, such employments of cinema are characterized as cultural conciliatory efforts (as opposed to purposeful publicity), trying to advance understanding of U.S. abroad.

According to Sanders (2011), this truly noteworthy connection between cinematic portrayal and U.S. diplomacy has become progressively imperative because of the ascent in argumentative universal relations and misshaped (frequently media-based) view of countries and societies around the world.

The ramifications of this relationship for diverse association are explored through the American Film Showcase (AFS), a newly created cultural diplomacy program originating from the U.S. Department of State's (DOS) in collaboration with the University of Southern California (USC).

The AFS sends films and their producers around the globe, leading screenings and holding classes/workshops for foreign viewers to:

- Improve foreign understanding of U.S. society (comprehensively);
- Raise awareness of the American audience on current social issues (for example migration, destitution, sexism, climate change and global warming);
- Cultivate a discourse about such issues to help mitigate them;
- Spread information about U.S. filmmaking through classes/workshops on distribution, computerized innovation, promoting the films, advertisement and so forth. (Peters, 2015)

Some examples of the use of film for cultural diplomacy put together by the Academy for Cultural Diplomacy includes:

Hiroshima Mon Amour 1959, (Understanding the concept of memory in different cultures):

This was a screenplay written by Marguerite Duras, directed by Alain Resnais, and won the Special Jury Prize at the Cannes Film Festival in 1959. It acted as a major motivator for the Nouvelle Vague (French New Wave) cinematic movement. The film explores different cultures by focusing on a fling between a Japanese architect and a French actress filming in

Hiroshima. It explores the obstacles encountered when we try to reconcile disparate cultures.

The film director uses the fictional situation of the two lovers to critique the impossibility of truly knowing and understanding one another; the backdrop of the atomic bomb being dropped on Hiroshima underlines the disparity between Western and Japanese recollections of the atrocity. The film explores the universal themes of love, war, and culture, but should be viewed as a plea for peace and the abolition of warfare. As such, it demonstrates the importance of international cooperation, showing the dangers of what can happen when socio-cultural conflicts are allowed to develop and mutate.

Seven Samurai, (Power is in sharing):

Set in 16th century Japan, it tells the story of a poor farming village, subjected to an annual rampage by marauding bandits. A ronin, answers a farming village's request for protection and he recruits six other Samurai to help. They protect and teach the villagers how to defend themselves, in exchange for only three small meals a day.

However, within this simple story we can see a magnificent tale involving self-sacrifice, honor, bonding and sympathy for the poor. This movie still teaches the world a set of invaluable lessons useful for those involved in public diplomacy/public policy, including:

- Taking action.
- Striving for unity.
- Facing problem timely.
- Learning strategies to tackle crisis.
- Engaging skillful people with knowhow to assist resolving crisis.
- Seeing the goal and following it through.
- Directing all the efforts to the shared cause, which serves as guiding force.
- Acting with honor and dignity.

Akira Kurosawa's 1954 classic, 'Seven Samurai' is still considered as the most forward-thinking piece ever created. An international hit, which Kurosawa followed it up with several more - Yojimbo, Sanjuro, The Hidden Fortress - all using his signature actor Toshiro Mifune.

Its appeal lies in emotions and mythologies not only specific to feudal Japan, but which strikes a universal chord worldwide – even today.

Seven Samurai established an elegant cinematic template for promoting concepts such as 'Power is in sharing', 'Teaching sustainability/Self-sufficiency', 'Expression of intent', 'Reliability', 'Human dignity', and 'Benevolence'.

Kurosawa's Samurai and martial epic movies facilitated the globalization of martial arts and paved the way for actors such as Bruce Lee and Sonny Chiba to further export Asian cultures to the West through their movies in the 70s.

The plot of Seven Samurai influenced movies' pop culture, and has been adopted not just in 'The Magnificent Seven' (Hollywood made two versions, one in 1960, the other in 2016), but in science fictions such as 'Battle Beyond the Stars', 'Rogue One' and of course it influenced George Lucas's 'Star Wars'.

Pocahontas (A native American and a British settle breaking down prejudices) :

Pocahontas recounts the narrative of a local American and an English pioneer who defeat cultural limits and become hopelessly enamored. The two cultural gatherings (the locals and the pioneers) doubt one another at first; however, Pocahontas and John Smith gradually build up a companionship that demonstrates the recently held preferences were misconstrued. Through connection and an extended comprehension of each other's way of life, they turn out to be more tolerating one another despite of differences.

Invictus, 2009 (Nelson Mandela uses sport to win a match against Apartheid and Cultural hatred):

Nelson Mandela's administration in South Africa was still separated by post-politically sanctioned racial segregation issues in his first year as president.

His hardest test was to transform a formerly supremacist country into a culturally modern and tolerant land. Politically-sanctioned racial segregation was with no doubt an authoritative product; however, not in the hearts of the general population.

Mandela, who realized that games could play an important role in disposing racial bias, supports Rugby World Cup, and uses sport to close the racial gap between blacks and whites. Invictus, a movie by Clint Eastwood, is a motion picture about how sports can unite and move an entire Country.

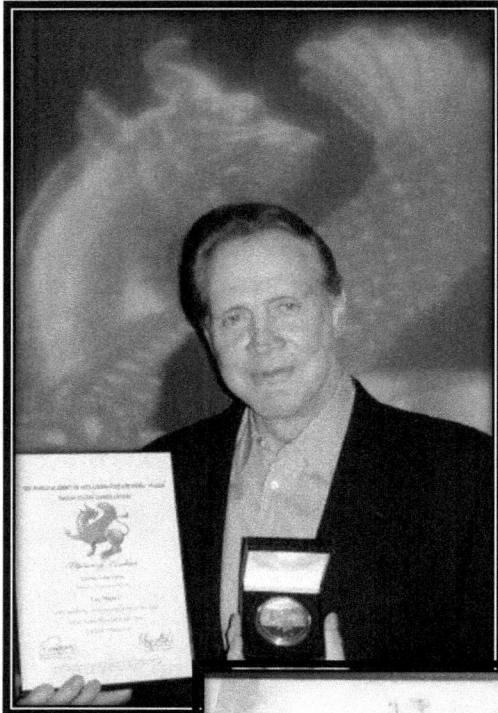

Lee Majors, WAALM Award Winning Actor.

Shohreh Aghdashloo, WAALM & Emmy Award Winning Actress.

Where do we go now? 2012 (Muslim and Christian Women United to end absurdity of the war):

This Lebanese film recounts the account of a gathering of Muslim and Christian ladies who plot to stop the continuous battle between their spouses.

In the wake of hearing news about the ascent of religious contradiction in the neighbouring regions, a nearby clash starts when the Christians find a harmed cross in their congregation, and the Muslims locate a polluted mosque. The ladies arrange series of a progressive, yet clever occasions to divert the men from proceeding with the battling.

CHAPTER 3

Theater and Performing Arts for Cultural Diplomacy

In his book, 'The Intercultural Performance Reader', Patrice Pavis states:

"It is in the search for extra-European inspiration—Asian, African, South American—that the genre of intercultural theater has every chance of prosperity, much more than in the co-operations between European countries, which often restrict themselves." (Pavis,1996, p.19)

Nowadays, art has its own personality rather than conforming to other rules and regulations; therefore, theater has found the chance to revolutionize itself, so that audiences could better grasp it.

In a constantly changing environment, theater is able to do more for the good of humanity. As opposed to the motion picture, it leaves a long-lasting impression on human's mind and it is indeed a practical extension to intercultural collaboration. (DeCarli, 2010 p.64)

Patrick Monahan, from Ireland - Performing Stand up Comedy at WAALM.

Prof. Najfar of Mozarteum Salzburg, from Austria - Performing Classical Flute.

Interrelations and collaborative efforts can be fostered if theater and performing arts can be expressed cross culturally on national or international stages.

Some countries have tailored their national policy and their communities to use theater and performing arts for cultural diplomacy. Examples include: 'The UK's Council for the Encouragement of Music and the Arts (CEMA)'; 'The Ministry of Culture and Communications of France'; 'The State of Germany and its Cultural Foundation'; and 'The United States' National Endowment of the Arts (NEA)'. Moreover, the same nations organize festivals and events for cultural diplomacy. (DeCarli, 2010 p.65)

The followings are some of the programs, organizations and festivals worthy of especial note:

A) Programs / Organizations:

Canada: Canoo (formerly known as Cultural Access Pass)

According to Institute for Canadian Citizenship's website, "New Canadian citizens explore, travel, and discover Canada during their first year of citizenship with the ICC's Canoo App. The only program of its kind in the world, Canoo provides members with free admission to more than 1,400 of Canada's premier cultural attractions and discounts on travel.

Powered by a passionate and committed national network, the Institute for Canadian Citizenship (ICC) delivers programs and special projects that inspire inclusion, create opportunities to connect, and encourage active citizenship.

The ICC is a national charity co-founded and co-chaired by The Right Honourable Adrienne Clarkson and John Ralston Saul. The Institute for Canadian Citizenship is committed to ensuring equal access and participation for all people." (www.icc-icc.ca)

United Kingdom: CEMA

According to the Arts Council of England (n.d), this council (Council of the Encouragement of Music and Arts) began in the United Kingdom in 1940. It was used as a tool to foster and promote British Culture during the time of the war. It was strongly supported by John Maynard Keynes who managed to secure government funds for arts without it becoming a government enterprise. After his death, the council was incorporated by Royal charter and became the Arts Council of England. This council has been through many upheavals and funding issue overtime but as stated on their charter website, their main objective is:

"…to develop and improve the knowledge, understanding and practice of the arts, to increase the accessibility of the arts to the public throughout Great Britain and to advise and co-operate with departments of Government, local authorities and other bodies on any matters concerned, whether directly or indirectly, with the foregoing objects". (The Arts Council of England, 1960)

France: Ministry of Culture

This Ministry was created by Charles de Gaulle in 1959 and bureau specialist in charge of securing arts inside France as well as abroad. He was preceded by Andre Malraux who made a great effort to incorporate the rights to culture in the French constitution thus protecting Charles de Gaulle's legacy and demonstrating the significance of post-war France. He equally fought for the democratization of access to culture. As a result, multiple regional centers were born as well as motivation throughout France to support the arts. The Union of Theater Europe was founded by former France's Minister of Culture, Jack Lang in 1990. His aim was to make a theater that eased the incorporation of the Europe, especially during globalization. The Minister of Culture and Diversity in France is equally responsible for the Avignon theater festival. (www.culture.gouv.fr)

Germany: The States & The German Cultural Council

Germany has a long past with performing arts showcasing culture. It needed to conquer numerous obstacles to fix the harm that was done in World War I and particularly World War II. Germany has limited federal approach about arts; however, there is an arrangement with every state for federal support and funding.

As culture was reassessed under Hitler, it has been re-evaluated again to give a progressively modest character to Germany. (James, 1998 p.152-160) The government therefore does its best to fund arts based on the states' needs.

For instance, Germany's public arts funding, enables Germany to have 23 times more full-time ensemble symphonies per national capita and more full-time musical jobs and orchestras.

63

Germany has a well-established theater network with over 300 theaters, as well as 130 professional orchestras that are funded by the public system and the states. (www.artsjournal.com)

"The German Cultural Council serves as a contact in politics and administration in the states, at a national level and in the European Union. Its stated goal is to encourage discussions on cultural policy at all levels of politics and to defend the freedom of art, publications, and information. Central issues of the recent years addressed by this council include the *protection of cultural goods, copyright, free trade agreements,* *'gender equality', 'cultural integration', 'economic and social issues'* or the issue threatening cultural institutions by introducing a Red List.

The Deutsches Zentrum des Internationalen Theaterinstituts (German Center of the International Theater Institute) is also a member and has made the mutual understanding of theater cultures of the world its goal. Along with books, dossiers, addenda, and studies, the German Cultural Council publishes the journal "politik & kultur" quarterly." (Lewy, H. 2017, https://conflict-zones.reviews/)

United States: NEA

According to the First Annual Report of the National Council on the Arts, congress created the National Endowments for the Arts in 1964, in order to encourage the nation's cultural progress.

The aim of this agency was to support and extend the participation of people in the arts by opening doors for more expert practices.

Today, this goal hasn't changed much, but the NEA aims to support excellence in arts, both new and old. It strives to convey arts to all American and providing leadership in arts education.

The NEA also started an international literary exchange program in 2007. The exchange was initially amongst the U.S, Ireland and Russia but expanded to Egypt and Morocco as well. (National Endowment for the Arts, 2008)

B) Festivals / Events:

United Kingdom: LIFT

LIFT makes remarkable cultural events, festivals and encounters for London. Enlivened by the internationalism and multiculturalism of the city, it welcomes artists from around the globe to interface with Londoners and make theater that lifts the audience out of the ordinary. It changes the audiences' comprehension of themselves, networks and general surroundings. It endeavors to be a pioneer in building up another participatory culture, new cultural thoughts and inventive employment of open space. (www.liftfestival.com)

France: Festival d'Avignon

This festival began in 1947 under the direction of Jean Vilar and has become the future of theatrical diplomacy. According to DeCarli, (2010, p.76) every year people are exposed to performances that represent different cultures. The festivals bring an education to people that instead of watching on a television they can experience it in real life.

UK and Canada: WAALM:

The World Academy of Arts, Literature and Media – WAALM is a registered non-for-profit organization in England and Wales, with satellite representatives in North America.

WAALM supports, develops, and promotes the dramatic and fine arts, music, creative writing and poetry, as well as professional journalism and media productions. It regularly identifies and rewards excellence, and benefits the public, by means of awarding events through which the public gets the opportunity to learn more about cross-cultural activities through international media and events that are open to public.

WAALM is one of the top ten awarding bodies in the world, which recognizes cultural productions for their merits, rather than their commercial values.

As a non-profit, independent and secular organization, WAALM stands for Cultural Diplomacy; it promotes cross-cultural activities, conferences and humanitarian efforts.
(www.facebook.com/waalmawards)

WAALM Ensemble and Leading Classical Performers.

WAALM Supported International Youth Ballet.

68

CHAPTER 4

Fine Art for Cultural Diplomacy

Fine art can assume an essential role in a nation's public diplomacy. Fine art can create a chance for nations to connect and rise above their political contrasts through show cases.

The advancement of fine art by individual nations comprises the expansive idea of cultural diplomacy, which equally can be found in other forms of cultural articulations, such as writing, music or even sport. (Keith, 2014 www.diplomatmagazine.nl)

Here are a few examples:

The Venice Biennale Universal Art Show is a prominent fine arts occasion that pulled in more than 475,000 guests in 2013. While the estimation was for ten countries to participate, seventy-eight nations effectively joined the show. Including artists from Angola, Bahamas, Côte d'Ivoire, Kuwait, Maldives, and Paraguay. (Keith, 2014, www.diplomatmagazine.nl)

Other fine arts occasions are exhibitions, which try to incorporate different works of art from different sources and artists. In the 1950s, the United States Information Agency (USIA) sponsored a photographic show or exhibition called the Family Man. This exhibition was done in the Museum of modern art in New York City, but the USIA displayed it in 91 locations in 39 countries. It included 503 photographs from 237 professional and amateur photographers and showed glimpses of everyday human life at different stages.

Very few of these photos were politically inclined and were coloured. This demonstrated diversity in the American culture and attracted a large number of people who learned about different backgrounds of humanity from this exhibition. (Nicholas, 2008, p.39-40)

Another exhibition organized by the United States Department in February 2002 was entitled Pictures from Ground Zero. The showcase included 27 pictures, specifying the September 11 assaults by Joel Meyerowitz that flowed, with the sponsorship of international safe havens and departments, to 60 countries.

The presentation was to shape and keep up the general population's memory of the assault and its repercussions. The presentation tried to demonstrate the human side of the catastrophe. The presentation additionally demonstrated an account for recuperation from misery and agony through perseverance.

Often outside US where the showcase was run, the exhibition was customized for the public. For instance, relatives of the individuals who passed on in the Towers were regularly invited to the openings (Liam, 2003, p.315-323) This showcase around the world, helped US to prevent the world from overlooking or forgetting the tragedy.

"Culture is the arts elevated to a set of beliefs"

Thomas Wolfe

CHAPTER 5

Aboriginal Arts for Cultural Diplomacy

Aboriginal art is generally accepted to be the longest-proceeding artistic custom on the planet: Australia flaunts in canvases equivalent in age to those of Europe's Lascaux and Altamira, with a rich emblematic dialect that beholds back to a primordial 'dreamtime'. Ancient artists made their 'campaigns' from bark, expelling it from trees and levelling it before treating it with the sticky liquids from orchids, making a glue dark or red foundation.

They got their palettes from red and yellow ochres, ground up and blended with water. Charcoal and kaolin earth served for making highly contrasting hues. In any case, generally of its 30,000-year presence it was the backwoods, known just to itself. (Myroslava, 2017, www.odessareview.com)

Exporting exhibitions of Aboriginal art to advance Australia's universal way of life as a tolerant and illuminated country has a moderately short history. Seen with nonchalance or disregard at home by Australian art historical centers until the mid-1980s, Aboriginal art is currently consistently exhibited abroad as the nation's overwhelming art frame and driving cultural fare, equipped for speaking to Australia in the zone of cultural diplomacy. (Gay, 2014, p.18-31)

The government swift in perceiving the undiscovered cultural-diplomatic prospects of the country's first artistic yield. It wasn't long before the National Museum of Australia opened its doors, offering new material history. With this official grasp of aboriginal art, bark painting turned into a national image.

In the course of recent years, the Australian government has bought and repatriated many barks work of art from prior periods. A significant number of these were purchased by European ethnographers, voyagers, gatherers in the main portion of the twentieth century. (Myroslava, 2017, www.odessareview.com)

Today, Australia has accepted a policy of multiculturalism, which has given rise to equal rights to every single Australian native in education, work, social insurance, and equity, and tries to cleanse its immigration policy of racial segregation. Indigenous culture, having a place with only 1.5% of its populace, assumes an essential job in forming the nation's contemporary personality. Propelled onto the international stage, it fills in as both calling card and a contribution to world's legacy by a general public that regardless, remains particularly Anglo-Celtic at its center. (www.odessareview.com)

Aboriginal arts in Canada is another significant contribution to cultural exchange.

Totem Pole – Vancouver, Canada.

According to Canada Council and Kelly Hill of Hill Strategies: "Aboriginal culture touches all aspects of human being – from creation stories to medicine to our relationship with nature to sexuality to creativity to food. This knowledge, going back millennia, informs principles of health, healing, justice, education, ecology, social work and many others. Historical knowledge also "has a direct connection to identity and art practice." (www.canadacouncil.ca; www.hillstrategies.com)

Working with communities, "many artists have important connections with their communities and sometimes this connection is evident both in their work and its impact within the community." Probing further the situation of Aboriginal artists, the report indicates that "many, though certainly not all Aboriginal artists face the quandary of hybridity – working within two ancestries, two traditions or two aesthetics."

In recent times, "there has been a resurgence of Aboriginal artistic production", with Aboriginal artists reviving and re-imagining traditional images, dances and songs in a contemporary context. Many contemporary artists "have used their work to discuss, to examine and to re-interpret the effects of colonial history". (www.canadacouncil.ca; www.hillstrategies.com)

The future tendencies in Aboriginal society and art is promising:

- There are increasing levels of formal education among Aboriginal youth.
- Important exchanges of knowledge and strategies are taking place among Indigenous peoples.
- New and emerging technologies are having an impact on Aboriginal artists and communities.

- There are more Aboriginal artists with mixed roots "creating hybrid art forms".

- Through the production of their work, artists are contributing to Aboriginal healing from the impacts of colonization.

Of course, the above tendencies are not free from challenges: Infrastructure, new arts awareness (and new audiences), critical discourse, and Indigenization (i.e., reclaiming, re-appropriating and re-imagining Aboriginal ways of being in the world) are among the issues facing Aboriginal arts in Canada." (www.canadacouncil.ca ; www.hillstrategies.com)

One of the remarkable centers facilitating Indigenous arts and cultural exchange is 'Bill Reid Gallery', situated in downtown Vancouver, British Columbia. It was named after the acclaimed Haida artist, Bill Reid (1920 – 1998), who was a master goldsmith, carver, sculptor, writer, broadcaster and spokesman.

The Bill Reid Gallery is home to the Simon Fraser University Bill Reid Collection and exhibits contemporary Indigenous Art of the Northwest Coast of North America. It is Canada's only public gallery dedicated to contemporary Indigenous Art of the Northwest Coast. (www.billreidgallery.ca)

'The Raven and the First Men', by Haida Artist, Bill Reid
Museum of Anthropology at UBC, Vancouver, Canada.

CHAPTER 6

Poetry for Cultural Diplomacy

Poetry is often used as a means of communication in political issues because of its elegant, gentle, yet persuasive function. Its sophisticated character makes it suitable to influence public opinion. It often presents a rational argument, accompanied by emotions.

The role of poetry in cultural diplomacy can be traced back to 18th century, when many diplomats used poetry to enhance their interactions. For example, "Willem van Haren (1710-1768), whose political poems played an important role in the negotiations of international political relations during the War of the Austrian Succession." (Jensen and Corporaal, 2016)

Even recently poetry has been used by politicians to reach out to the public. In October 2014 during a keynote speech on the status of nuclear negotiations with Iran, U.S. chief nuclear negotiator, Wendy Sherman cited a verse by the great Persian poet Saadi: *"Have patience; all things are difficult before they become easy."* The citation appeared to be an attempt by Sherman to reach out to Iranians by showing respect for their culture and love of poetry. (www.rferl.org)

The U.S. President, Barack Obama has also recited Persian poetry in his efforts to engage Iran, during his media appearances and video messages to Iranians.

In his 2011 message for Nowruz, the Persian New Year (March 21st), Obama recited a verse from Simin Behbahani (1927 - 2014), a WAALM award-winning poet, who repeatedly faced pressure from Iranian authorities.

"Old, I may be, but, given the chance, I will learn. I will begin a second youth alongside my progeny. I will recite the Hadith of love of a country with such fervor as to make each word bear life, " Obama said in his citation of Behbahani. (www.rferl.org)

Obama's 2013 Nowruz message also included a verse by the 14th century poet Hafez, whose book of poetry is part of almost every household in Iran.

"Plant the tree of friendship that bears the fruit of fulfillment; uproot the sapling of enmity that bears endless suffering," Obama said in his Persian New Year video greetings. (www.rferl.org)

Poetry can also become a powerful tool for promoting understanding and tolerance among nations.

During the completion of the United Nations complex in New York City in 1952, The UN decides to permanently display a few significant Human Rights symbols inside the building. Among several items, we can see a poem on the top of the Hall of Nations entrance door. (www.visit.un.org)

Many scholars from several nations get assigned by the UN to find out the best available written poem describing the UN's vision, mission and values. After studying the world's poetry, the team of scholars select Saadi's 13th century passage:

"Children of Adam are the limbs of one

Since all, at first, from the same essence came

When time afflicts a limb with pain

The other limbs at rest cannot remain

If thou feel not for other's misery

A human being is no name for thee"

Saadi Shirazi (simply known as Saadi) was one of the major Persian poets and literary men of the medieval period (1210 - 1292). He is recognized for the quality of his writings and for the depth of his social and moral thoughts.

I also borrowed and adapted the same Saadi's verse for my song titled: 'To whom It May Concern', performed by a Canadian singer of excellence, Kate Todd, which says:

"...Human beings are members of a whole
In creation of one essence and soul

If one member is afflicted with pain
Other members uneasy will remain

If we have no sympathy for human pain
The name of human we cannot retain..."

I created that song to promote tolerance and understanding around the world, and to highlight the UN's International Day of Social Justice and Equality (20th February).

"The pursuit of social equality and justice for all, is at the core of many UN affiliated global mission to promote human dignity. Social equality and justice are an underlying principle for a peaceful and prosperous coexistence within and among nations. All of us can uphold the principles of social equality and justice, when we promote gender equality or the rights of indigenous peoples and migrants. We all can advance social equality and justice, when we remove barriers that people face because of gender, age, race, ethnicity, religion, culture or disability." (www.un.org)

CHAPTER 7

TV Shows for Cultural Diplomacy

Conan Without Borders

Conan Christopher O'Brien is an American television host, comedian, writer, and producer. He is best known for hosting several late-night talk shows since 1983, the longest-working of all current late-night talk show hosts in the United States. Since 2010, he has hosted Conan on the cable channel TBS. (www.tbs.com/shows/conan) O'Brien was born in Brookline, Massachusetts, and raised in an Irish Catholic family. (https://en.wikipedia.org)

'Conan Without Borders' are especial episodes filmed abroad. These episodes did not follow the traditional format and were not filmed before an audience. Instead, they involve O'Brien being followed by a camera crew as he focuses more on the normal life of the locals and visiting cultural locations, all while improvising to provide comedy. Both entertaining and educational, 'Conan Without Borders' never avoided sensitive topics and effectively established dialogue through television.

March 1, 2017: Conan went to Mexico: This visit was made in response to actions and the effort made by President Donald Trump to build a wall across the southern border.

September 19, 2017: Conan Without Borders is taped in Israel and he even visited the West Bank. This episode was made in response to Trump associate, Jared Kushner's attempts to further the Israeli-Palestinian peace process.

January 27, 2018: Conan visited Haiti: his visit was in response to President Donald Trump's alleged description of the country and parts of Africa as "sh--holes". (Brett, 2018 www.thehill.com)

Emigrants Monument - Bremerhaven, Germany.

CHAPTER 8

Digital for Cultural Diplomacy

Once the main objective of culture was to create arts & literature and assist the promotion of such productions through exhibitions and performances, it no longer serves as the prime-serving goal for culture.

Culture is having a diplomatic role in global governance and in this respect "Cultural Diplomacy" is increasingly playing an important role in promoting liberal and democratic values. It fosters dialogue and democratic participation. It facilitates human development, expansion of education, human rights, freedom of thought and expression. It also assists recognition and understanding of value-oriented causes and missions.

The importance of Cultural Diplomacy is mentioned in the Lisbon Treaty and the UNESCO convention: "Culture should be mainstreamed and be an element of every program from students and teachers to journalists and artists exchange". (https://en.unesco.org)

With the new crucial role that blogs, podcasts, and social networking sites are playing, the EU parliament is now emphasizing on new strategies to utilize digital mediums to further cultural diplomacy.

Interactions over the Internet could break censorship and taboos, help foster dialogue and engage people in democracy, and all these are part of culture.

In my view 'Digital Diplomacy' is on its way to enhance perceiving and prevailing Cultural Diplomacy around the world.

Changes in the world political landscape, globalization, and the new digital communication technologies have narrowed the distance between countries, and between leaders and their nations. This has given rise to 'Digital Diplomacy' more than ever.

According to a recent report by Elizabeth Bloodgood and Tristan Masson (2018), "Internet accessibility and usage expands worldwide, particularly among young people. A little over a decade after its creation, Twitter attracts 330 million monthly active users. Nearly 80% of users are from outside the United States and can choose from more than 40 operating languages.

With a few more years under its belt, Facebook attracts 1.4 billion daily active users and over 2.1 billion monthly active users.

More than 80% of users come from outside the US and Canada. In fact, the digital divide between developed and developing regions is narrowing. From 2013 to 2015, the median rate of Internet used by adults in developing countries rose from 45 to 54%, while smartphone ownership rose from 13 to 37%.

Once connected to the Web, users from developing areas are more frequent users of social media like Twitter and Facebook than their European and North American counterparts. Heads of government and/or state have Twitter accounts, along with their ministerial colleagues in foreign affairs, trade and international development. Each of these ministries typically has a bureaucratic arm that operates its own Twitter accounts.

86

Of course, the same tools that allow governments to speak directly to citizens around the world and increase space for under-represented voices in policy debates also provide podiums for the spread of global populism and amplify discontent around the real or imagined impacts of globalization. With the rise of social media, governments no longer control the content of international diplomacy."
(www.policyoptions.irpp.org)

SECTION THREE

Cultural Diplomacy: The Essential Quality & Skills

Who is a Cultural Diplomat?

A Cultural Diplomat is a contributor of artistic or creative industry, who on top of their creative artisanship can be sensitive in dealing with people from different backgrounds. An individual who can achieve peaceful resolutions or facilitate discussion and dialogue through cross-cultures or cultural exchange. A cultural figure who does not take sides in a conflict, but fosters collaborations and ties to advance mutual and national interests by helping all parties to resolve their differences free from violence.

The Knotted Gun Sculpture by Carl Fredrick Reutersward,
United Nations Building, Manhattan, NYC, USA

The Key Qualities of a Cultural Diplomat

- **Openness:** willing to learn about the world, its people and their cultures.

- **Fairness:** knowing that no culture is superior to another, they are just different.

- **Dignity**: treating everyone with respect and consider them as an individual. Conducting their affairs with integrity, projecting self-respect and appreciating gravity of an occasion or situation.

Additionally, Cultural Diplomats are *'verbally fluent and concise'*. They *'pay attention'*, *'speak only when necessary'*, and *'keep their comments brief'*. They have *'empathy'* and they *'show affinity'* when needed.

They are *'tactful'*, *'insightful'*, and *'analytical'* and they have *'strategic thinking'*. They believe that *'power is in sharing'* and they use all their materials at their disposal to establish common ground and mutual understanding.

They are resolved in their private lives, have *'compassion'*, *'determination'* and *'confidence'*. The most successful Cultural Diplomats are those with *'perseverance'* and *'humble attitude'*.

The Skillsets of a Cultural Diplomat

A successful Cultural Diplomat has the following skillsets:

- **Soft Skills:** This includes people, social, and communication skills; positive attitudes; professional career attributes; social and emotional intelligence; socio-economics and political awareness.

- **Public Advocacy:** Ability to act to influence social, political, and economic systems through dialogue and cultural exchange. Identifying important causes and policies which benefit the public or a particular group and supporting them by implementing cultural tools and applications.

- **Organizational Skills:** Facilitating local, national and international relations. Prioritizing and ordering tasks effectively and efficiently. Applying a systematic approach to achieving objectives with appropriate use of resources.

- **Leadership:** To assume responsibility and persist to realize the goal. To positively influence group's activity, direction and opinion and motivate others to participate in the cause and to contribute collaboratively.

- **Negotiation:** As an adviser and cultural diplomacy advocate, I attended and conducted numerous international negotiations and what I experienced was that effective negotiators are highly adaptable. They do not stick to static strategies all the time.

Skillful negotiators are highly vigilant throughout the process of negotiation – from beginning to the end, and they are constantly absorbing information on their counterparts. Absorbing information such as their:

- Habits.
- Speaking patterns.
- Presentation patterns.
- Personal style.

Skilled negotiators monitor themselves as well and make certain that they avoid showing reactions to choices that their counterpart presents.

'Adaptability' is a key factor in successful negotiation.

In addition, a Cultural Diplomat, who is advocating public diplomacy should know:

- **History:** Knowing history on its own does not provide you with a single policy, nor motives for prescriptions in a given current circumstance; however, it does illuminate choices for decisions. Remember, you can predict the future behavior by studying the past.
- **Values:** To communicate effectively and harmoniously with people of other cultures, you need to fully understand their system of values, political and religious beliefs, economic and infrastructure circumstances and respect their differences and cultural environments.

Build a Bridge to Communicate - Illustrated by: Frits Ahlefldt - C.C.

*"The supreme art of war is to
subdue the enemy without fighting."*

Sun Tzu

ABOUT AUTHOR

Mosi Dorbayani is a Canadian entrepreneur, executive adviser, educator, coach and consultant in international management and strategic leadership. He is author of 21 books and is a well-published international songwriter.

His executive experience, leading and collaborating with staff from 20 nationalities have equipped him with a global strategic understanding on the importance of cultural diversity and human capital.

As a Goodwill Ambassador, Mosi serves several UN affiliated organizations close to his heart and promotes education of Universal Declaration of Human Rights – UDHR and Cultural Diplomacy around the world.

Mosi is a member of The Academic Council on The United Nations System, and UNA, New York, and is the recipient of 2010 Human Rights Hero Awards, at the United Nations in Geneva.

/MosiDorbayani

95

ALSO, FROM THIS AUTHOR:

❖ **Message Song: Delivering Important and Powerful Messages Through Lyrics and Music** – ISBN: 978-0-9940842-5-5

❖ **The Role of Music and Lyrics in Social Behavior: An Investigative Short Essay** – ASIN: B07LFQQL3X

❖ **Business Samurai: Skills & Strategies for Leaders and Entrepreneurs** – ISBN: 978-0-9940842-3-1

❖ **Think About It** – ISBN: 978-0-9940842-2-4

❖ **Concise HR & Personnel** – ISBN: 963 212 096 5

❖ **Concise Economics** – ISBN: 963 212 093 0

❖ **Successful Business Organization** – ISBN: 963 210 234 7

❖ **Successful Management** – ISBN: 963 210 233 9

❖ **Successful Leadership** – ISBN: 963 204 821 0

❖ **Moderation Management Enlightened with Philosophy** – ISBN: 963 210 699 7

❖ **Hidden** – ISBN 978-0-9940842-0-0

❖ **Kojido Sogo Bujutsu: The Way of Persistence in Martial Arts** – ISBN 978-0-9940842-1-7

Mosi Dorbayani

MESSAGE SONG

DELIVERING IMPORTANT AND POWERFUL MESSAGES THROUGH LYRICS AND MUSIC

THE ROLE OF MUSIC & LYRICS IN SOCIAL BEHAVIOR

Essay by:

Mosi Dorbayani

WAALM PUBLICATIONS

KATE TODD
TO WHOM IT MAY CONCERN

Songwriter: Mosi Dorbayani & Saadi
Orchestration: Amarita
Producer: Peter Linseman

20th Feb
Highlighting UN's World Day of Social Equality & Justice

/katetoddentertainment   /MosiDorbayani   /PeterLinseman

@WaalmAwards   http://www.musicmentorproductions.com

Translation of Saadi's verse M. Aryanpoor

Facilitated by: WAALM

MusicMentor
Productions

'To Whom It May Concern'

By: Canadian Singer/ Musician /Actress: Kate Todd

Highlighting UN's World Day of Social Equality & Justice

Available to View, Stream and Download from:

YouTube, Spotify and iTunes

Learn more about Kate Todd at:
www.facebook.com/katetoddentertainment
www.musicmentorproductions.com

99

Songwriter: Mosi Dorbayani
Orchestration: Makai Symphony

WAALM Productions

'Chase the Sun'

By: Japanese-British Soprano, Dolly Thompson

Celebrating UN's International Day of Peace

Available to Stream and Download from:

Spotify and iTunes

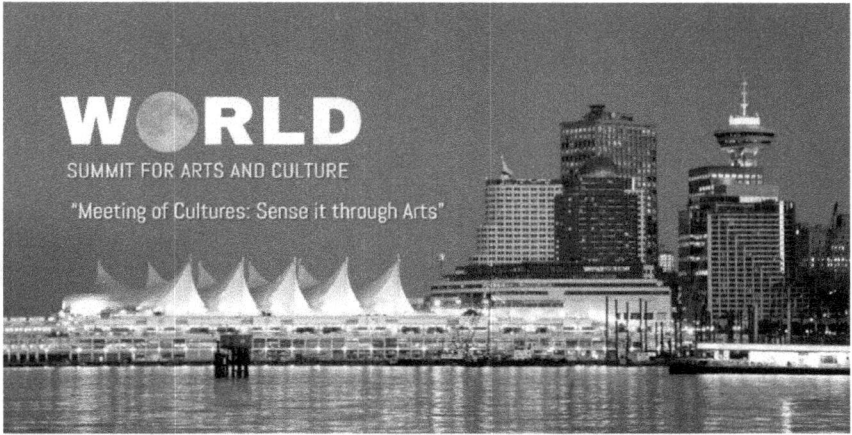

Under the directorship of this author,

WAALM and School of Cultural Diplomacy, Present:

WORLD SUMMIT FOR ARTS AND CULTURE – VANCOUVER, BC, CANADA

The theme of the summit:

"Meeting of Cultures: Sense it through Arts".

The summit explores how the arts can help foster intercultural dialogue and social cohesion. Symposiums, workshops and round-table discussions are held over a three-day summit. The first day's event focuses on theoretical and historical issues; the second day's sessions focus on practical ideas that could be catalyzed at the summit, and the third day is allocated to 'performing arts', 'live stages', 'shows', 'galleries', and 'awards' etc.

Areas of Discussion:

- Issues pertinent to the future of arts and culture in the world would be discussed. Questions like: how do we continue these discussions in our own countries? how do we advocate for the arts nationally and internationally?

- Other topics on the agenda include: how public arts policy can contribute towards creating decent jobs; the importance of intercultural dialogue; art as an instrument for public good; freedom of expression; the global economic downturn; art in conflict and war zones; climate change, mental and health care.

- The summit also acts as a platform to examine various ways in which countries can support the arts: It aims to resolve how the arts can fit into a world where people are culturally divided and how they can be used to build multicultural societies and foster social cohesion or development between people of different backgrounds.

Extension:

The summit's dedicated website/social pages would bring the world summit's presentations, workshop videos, and video lectures to the public for FREE further education and streaming. A dedicated team of 250 cross-cultural and public policy enthusiasts would moderate online live feeds, discussions, and Q&A through social media platforms.

Estimation:

Over 750 official delegates, from 54 countries, with a global outreach of over 48 million.

Follow WAALM for news and updates:

/waalmawards

REFRENCES

Academy for Cultural Diplomacy (n.d). 'Film as Cultural Diplomacy', www.culturaldiplomacy.org/academy/index.php?en_film-as-cultural-diplomacy, accessed on Jan. 22nd 2019

Ackermann, K. (2018) 'State and Mainstream: The Jazz Ambassadors and The U.S. State Department', www.allaboutjazz.com, accessed on March 4th. 2019

Arts Council England: '1960s: A Time of Balance', http://www.artscouncil.org.uk/about-us/historyarts-council/1940-45/, accessed on Jan 28th 2019

Arts Council England: '1940–45: CEMA and the Beginning of the Arts Council, http://www.artscouncil.org.uk/about-us/history-arts-council/1940-45/ , accessed Jan 28th, 2019

Arndt, R. (2006) 'The first resort of kings. American cultural diplomacy in the twentieth century'. 2006,p.xviii, Washington, DC: Potomac Books.

Canada Council for Art, www.canadacouncil.ca, accessed Dec 15th, 2018

Carnes L. (2006, p.15) Losing Hearts and Minds?: Public Diplomacy and Strategic Influence in the Age of Terror (Westport, CT: Praeger Security International).

Cultural Learning Alliance, (2011) 'The Case for Cultural Learning: Key Research Findings'. http://culturallearningalliance.org.uk, accessed, Nov. 10th. 2018

Cummings, M. (2003, p.1) 'Cultural diplomacy and the United States government: a survey'. Washington, DC: Center for Arts and Culture.

DeCarli, Ashley M. (2010, p.64.65), Theater and cultural diplomacy: the role of the performing arts in how nations deal with each other. Monterey, California. Naval Postgraduate School https://calhoun.nps.edu/bitstream/handle/10945/5309/10Jun_DeCarli.pdf?sequence=1&isAllowed=y , accessed on Jan 2019

Esfandiari, G. (2014), 'In Washington, Poetry Diplomacy with Iran'. https://www.rferl.org/a/washington-poetry-diplomacy-with-iran/26654728.html, accessed Jan 2019

Finn, H. K, (2003) 'The Case for Cultural Diplomacy: Engaging Foreign Audiences', https://www.foreignaffairs.com/articles/2003-11-01/case-cultural-diplomacy-engaging-foreign-audiences. accessed Jan 7th. 2019

Gay McDonald, (2014) Aboriginal art and cultural diplomacy: Australia, the United States, and the 'Culture Warriors' exhibition, Journal of Australian Studies, 38:1, 18-31, DOI: 10.1080/14443058.2013.859168

Gardels, N. and Mike, M. (2009) 'American Idol After Iraq: Competing for Hearts and Minds in the Global Media Age'. Oxford, Chichester, UK, and Malden, MA: Wiley-Blackwell.

Hill Strategies Research Inc. www.hillstrategies.com, accessed Dec, 15 2018

ICD Academy for Cultural Diplomacy. '*Historical Acts of Cultural Diplomacy*', www.academy-for-cultural-diplomacy.de ,accessed on Jan 2019

Institute for Cultural Diplomacy, (n.d.), '*What is cultural diplomacy?*'.http://www.culturaldiplomacy.org/index.php?en_culturaldiplomacy , accessed on 20th, January 2019

James, P. (1998. p. 152–160) '*Modern Germany: Politics, Society and Culture*', Florence, KY: Routledge.

Jensen, L. and Corporral, M. (2016) '*Poetry as an Act of International Diplomacy: English translations of Willem van Haren's Political Poetry during the War of the Austrian Succession*', Journal for Eighteenth-Century Studies Vol. 39 No. 3 (2016) doi: 10.1111/1754-0208.12338.

Joseph S. Nye (2004, p.18) '*Soft Power: The Means to Success in World Politics*', Cambridge: Perseus Books

Keith D.(2014) '*Fine art and public diplomacy*': Diplomat Magazine, www.diplomatmagazine.nl/2014/03/02/fine-art-public-diplomacy/ , accessed on Jan 29th, 2019.

Kulturstiftung, Des Bundes, http://www.kulturstiftung-des-bundes.de/cms/en/stiftung/, accessed Jan 28th, 2019

Lewy, H. (2017), '*German Theater: Behind the scenes of its structures*', https://conflict-zones.reviews/german-theater-behind-scenes-structures, accessed April 2019

Liam, K., (2003, p.315-323.) "*Remembering September 11: Photography as Cultural Diplomacy,*" International Affairs 79, no. 2.

LIFT London International Festival of Theater (2009), http://www.liftfest.org.uk , accessed Jan 28th, 2019.

Louis B., (1999, p.677-8) *'Redefining Cultural Diplomacy: Cultural Security and Foreign Policy in Canada'* Political Psychology 20, no. 4:, doi:10.1111/0162-895X.00164.

MacCann, R.D., (1969). *'Film and Foreign Policy*: *The USIA, 1962-1967'*. Cinema Journal 9(1):23-42, http://www.jstor.org/stable/pdfplus/1225272.pdf?acceptTC=t rue , accessed on January 23rd 2019,

Mark. L. Sept/Oct 2002, p50-52) *'Diplomacy by Other Means'*, Foreign Policy 132.

Michael J. W. (2009, p. 74-75, 77, 82-87) *'Cultural Diplomacy, Political Influence, and Integrated Strategy, in Strategic Influence: Public Diplomacy, Counterpropaganda, and Political Warfare'* ed. Washington, DC: Institute of World Politics Press, 2009.

Muirhead and de Leeuw, Art and wellness, (2012), https://artshealthnetwork.ca, accessed Nov. 20th 2018

Music as Cultural Diplomacy (n.d), *'Music as cultural diplomacy'* Academy for Cultural Diplomacy http://www.culturaldiplomacy.org/academy/index.php?en_m acd_about , accessed on 25th, January 2019,

Myroslava. H, (2017) *'Australia's Aboriginal Art: A Human Rights Puzzle'*, The Odessa Review. http://odessareview.com/australias-aboriginal-art-human-rights-puzzle/, accessed on Jan 29th, 2019

National Endowment for the Arts (2008), Annual Report, Washington DC: United States Government

Narinehgh, (2012), *'Cultural Diplomacy and Film'*, Public and Cultural Diplomacy. https://publicandculturaldiplomacy3.wordpress.com/2012/03/09/cultural-diplomacy-and-film/ , accessed on Jan, 25th 2019

Nicholas J. C. (2008, p33) *"Public Diplomacy: Taxonomies and Histories,"* Annals of the American Academy of Political and Social Science 616..

Nicholas J. C., (2008, p. 39-40) *"Public Diplomacy: Taxonomies and Histories,"* Annals of the American Academy of Political and Social Science 616

Nye, J.S. Jr. (1990. p.32) *'Born to lead. The changing nature of American power'*. New York, NY: Basic Books.

Oana L. (2016) *'Music – one of the best ambassadors of Cultural diplomacy'*, Bulletin of the Transilvania University of Braşov - Supplement Series VIII: Performing Arts • Vol. 9 (58) No. 2. http://webbut.unitbv.ro/BU2016/Series%20VIII/Special%20Issue/19_Lianu%20Oana-corect.pdf, accessed on January 25th, 2019

Patrice, P., (1996, p.19) *'The Intercultural Performance Reader'*, New York: Routledg.

Peters, J. M. (2015). *'American Cinema as Cultural Diplomacy: Seeking International Understanding One Film at a Time'*. UCLA. ProQuest ID: Peters_ucla_0031D_13476. Merritt ID: ark:/13030/m5hf03jx.

https://escholarship.org/uc/item/11c6g3mk , accessed on Jan, 23rd 2019

Perrigo, B. (2017), 'How the U.S. Used Jazz as a Cold War Secret Weapon', Times. http://time.com/5056351/cold-war-jazz-ambassadors/, Accessed on the 25th of January 2019

Sanders, B. A. (2011) 'American Avatar: The United States in the Global Imagination', Washington, D.C.: Potomac Books

Samuels, B. (2018), "Conan to film show in Haiti in response to Trump's 's---hole' comments", https://thehill.com/blogs/in-the-know/369211-conan-to-film-show-in-haiti-in-response-to-trumps-shithole-comments, accessed January 16, 2019.

The Hill, https://thehill.com/blogs/in-the-know/369211-conan-to-film-show-in-haiti-in-response-to-trumps-shithole-comments, accessed on Feb. 10th 2019

USC Center on Diplomacy (2015) '10 Great Moments in Music Diplomacy'. www.uscpublicdiplomacy.org/story/10-great-moments-music-diplomacy , accessed on Jan 25th 2019

Walk in Style, (2014) 'Music for Humanity', https://musicforhumanity.wixsite.com/walkinstyle, accessed Jan. 2019

William O. (2004), "Marketplace of Ideas: But First, The Bill: A Personal Commentary On American and European Cultural Funding," ArtsJournal.com, www.artsjournal.com/artswatch/20040311-11320.shtml., accessed on Jan 28th 2019

Additional Websites Visited for Research on This Project:

www.culture.gouv.fr
www.kulturstiftung-des-bundes.de
www.diplomatmagazine.nl
www.tbs.com/shows/conan

Related Organizations for Academic Studies:

School of Cultural Diplomacy:
www.waalmdiplomacy.org

Institute for Cultural Diplomacy:
www.culturaldiplomacy.org

European Academy of Diplomacy:
https://diplomats.pl

North American Cultural Diplomacy Initiative:
www.culturaldiplomacyinitiative.com